I Love Me

BUILDING SELF-ESTEEM IN CHILDREN

Latrice Slaughter

Illustrated By:
Jay De Vance III

Copyright © 2015 by Latrice Slaughter
Los Angeles, California
All rights reserved
Printed and Bound in the United States of America

Published And Distributed By
Lioness Publishing
Email:livia.latrice@gmail.com

Packaging/Consulting
Professional Publishing House
1425 W. Manchester Ave. Ste B
Los Angeles, California 90047
323-750-3592
Email:www.professionalpublishinghouse@yahoo.com
www.Professionalpublishinghouse.com

Cover design: Jay De Vance, III
First printing March 2015
978-0-9961606-0-5
10987654321

No part of this book may be reproduced, stored in a retrieval system or transmitted in any form or by any means without the prior written permission of the publisher—except by a reviewer who may quote brief passages in a review to be printed in a newspaper, magazine or journal.
For inquiries contact: livia.latrice@gmail.com

Dedications

To my beautiful daughter Cairah. You are beautiful inside and out. Remember to shine from within first!

The best love story you will ever have is the one that involves you loving you.

Mother, here is the book you asked for. There are plenty more to follow. I love you.

Hi there! My name is Bree.
I am five years old, and I love me!

I love me. I love me.
I love me…me…me…me!

I will tell you why I love me the way that I do.

From the top of my head to the bottom of my shoe.

I have ten fingers and ten toes.

A head full of curly hair,

And a cute little button nose.

"Your skin is as smooth as a baby's bottom."

That's what my nana says when we play.

"And it's dark like the night sky."
That's why we dance
the night away.

Or at least until bedtime.

I love my eyes and I love my hair,
I love my color
And that's why I stare,

In the mirror sometimes because
I'm pleased, you see?

I would never want to be anyone else because I love me!

You should love you, too!
After all, there's only one you!

From the top of your head,
To the bottom of your shoe.

So the next time you're feeling sad
and not being the very best
you can be,

Just look in the mirror and say,
"I love me!"

www.ingramcontent.com/pod-product-compliance
Lightning Source LLC
Chambersburg PA
CBHW042142290426
44110CB00002B/90